STEPHEN DAVISON

ROAD RACERS

BLACKSTAFF PRESS

A RUTHLESS EMBRACE

During the early part of 2012, Ryan Farquhar and I spent a week in one another's company. Following the Scarborough Spring Cup, where Ryan was competing and I was taking pictures, we travelled together to the Isle of Man for a TT press launch. Long days turned into longer nights in hotel bars, leading to a great deal of discussion about road racing.

Having just celebrated his thirty-sixth birthday, the man who had won more races in Ireland than any other rider was considering his future in the sport. He had already ticked every box on a road racer's wish list, with victories at the North West 200, the Isle of Man TT, the Ulster Grand Prix, the Manx Grand Prix and the Scarborough Gold Cup, as well as dozens of Irish National race wins. Ryan could retire a happy and satisfied man.

It was surprising, then, to hear him struggle with the question of quitting racing. Night after night, he debated the pros and cons of the decision. The deep pleasure he found in racing and winning was being eroded by the hassles of dealing with officialdom and the long, tedious hours spent in the workshop preparing bikes.

Away from racing, Ryan had a loving wife, two beautiful daughters and a new home. A fledgling business enterprise offered a replacement for the income that road racing had provided. Free from the need to race to earn a living, Ryan worried that he was neglecting his young family and was beginning to question his commitment to the sport.

As we talked, though, it became clear that something else was troubling Ryan, something that would not allow him simply to walk away from racing. No matter the risks, he still felt hooked on the thrill that riding a motorcycle between trees and hedges at 150 mph and more provided. Road racers

refer to this simply as the 'buzz' and Ryan was held fast by the speed junkie's need for this adrenalin fix.

Nothing made him feel more alive.

In every discipline of motorcycle racing, riders find the limits by riding right up to the edge of control. If that fine line is crossed in the controlled environment of a short circuit, a rider can usually gather himself up from the gravel trap, dust down his leathers and be out in the next race. If that same line is crossed in a road race, it is a lottery whether a rider will ever see his family again.

Much has been done to make racing on closed public roads less dangerous and the removal of hedges and the placing of safety bales have improved the chances of a rider surviving a crash. But at high speed, danger looms at every turn and these precautions can only ever make things safer, never safe.

When probed on the perils that stare them in the face every time they jump on a bike, racers usually evade the question with dark humour. 'There's as much chance of being run over by a bus,' is a stock response, but in reality no one is more aware of the omnipresent dangers than those who race between the hedges. Ultimately, there is only one line of defence; the hope that it will never happen to them.

During the spring of 2012 Ryan Farquhar was beginning to question even this fragile refuge.

Although it may not have provided him with great riches, Ryan's road racing earnings in a successful season would have been measured in tens of thousands of pounds, considerably more than he could have earned in his previous day job servicing plant machinery. It had also brought a certain fame that had its own allure.

Winning had become a way of life and in 2012 Ryan was still enjoying victories almost every weekend. But he had to ride to his absolute limit, to the very edge of disaster, to obtain them. One slip and he would lose everything.

The fastest men are always those in the greatest danger and Ryan was well aware of what was at risk. During his career he had seen many of his closest rivals – men like Joey and Robert Dunlop, Richard Britton, Darran Lindsay and Martin Finnegan – pay the ultimate price as they gambled their lives in the same high-stakes game that he was playing. The law of averages suggested that to continue to do something so dangerous would have only one likely outcome.

It was painfully obvious that April week that Ryan could not resolve the battle that raged within between his fears and deepest desires. His hope of an external intervention was given desperate expression when he voiced the wish that road racing would be banned 'because then I could get out'.

Shocking as this sounded, the tragedy that was to finally force his hand was even more terrible.

Ryan was back in the Isle of Man in August 2012, standing on the pit wall at the Manx Grand Prix. He watched the road, waiting for a glimpse of the orange bike that his uncle, Trevor Ferguson, was riding in the Supertwins race. As the minutes ticked by and there was still no sign of Trevor, Ryan sensed something was wrong. When a rider goes missing his family fears the worst, hoping for the reprieve that news of a breakdown rather than an accident will bring – for Ryan and the Ferguson family, there was no reprieve. Trevor had crashed just a mile away, succumbing to his injuries at the scene.

A quiet and unassuming man who was always accompanied by his family at race meetings, Trevor Ferguson had taken Ryan to his first races. As a ten year old, Ryan had wheeled his uncle's bike to the grid and run errands for spanners and cleaning cloths. When he decided to have a go at racing himself, he did it on one of Trevor's old race bikes. For twenty years the pair had shared the journeys to races and the camaraderie of paddock life.

'Trevor saw me race my first race and I saw him race his last. We were together all along the way,' was how Ryan described their bond.

Although Ryan had seen many riders killed in crashes during his career, Trevor's death had, literally, brought it all home to him. There was no distance between him and the agony and despair he felt and had to watch in Trevor's family. Ryan immediately announced his retirement from the sport, explaining that he could not allow this horror to be visited upon his own family.

Although he has not raced since that day, Ryan has admitted that there have been times when he has been tempted to pull on his leathers and try again.

It is beyond the comprehension of ordinary mortals to understand what it is like to race a motorcycle at speeds the eye can scarcely see along roads lined with walls and telegraph poles that present the threat of instant death in the event of the smallest mistake. But road racers are no ordinary mortals and no matter how close we get to them, we remain eternal observers, always separated from the dangers by the sweet safety of being on the other side of the wall.

Even here, we feel the power of road racing to draw us in and hold us fast in its ruthless embrace.

JOEY DUNLOP'S WORKSHOP, BALLYMONEY, 2009

Joey Dunlop was killed in a crash during
a race in Estonia in 2000. At forty-eight
years of age, Dunlop was in his thirty-
first year of competition in a career that
would see him acknowledged as the
greatest road racer of all time. Although
he was contracted to the Honda factory
team, Dunlop prepared his own machines
in this small workshop behind his
Ballymoney home in County Antrim. It
has been preserved largely as he left it.

MICHAEL DUNLOP, ISLE OF MAN TT, 2011

When Michael Dunlop was learning the long and complex Mountain course at the start of his TT career, he followed a practice he had learned from his late father Robert.

Driving around the circuit at night, Robert used the headlights of his car to pick out braking markers and the places where he would start to peel into corners. He used a pot of paint and a brush to mark these spots so that they would give him his bearings when he was racing his bike at high speed around the 37.74 miles.

MID-ANTRIM 150, 2010

Rats watches and waits.

GUY MARTIN, ARMOY, 2011

Guy Martin takes a break from working on his Relentless Suzuki machines, which are parked in a farmyard that acts as the pits for the Armoy road races in County Antrim.

ISLE OF MAN TT, 2010

A marshal at Tower Bends reads the race programme before
the start of an evening practice session for the Isle of Man TT
in 2010. Almost five hundred marshals, all of whom are unpaid
volunteers, man the 37.74-mile course to ensure the safety of
riders and race fans.

KELLS, 2004

Race fans queue for breakfast on a street in Crossakiel
village in County Meath, the home of the Kells road races.

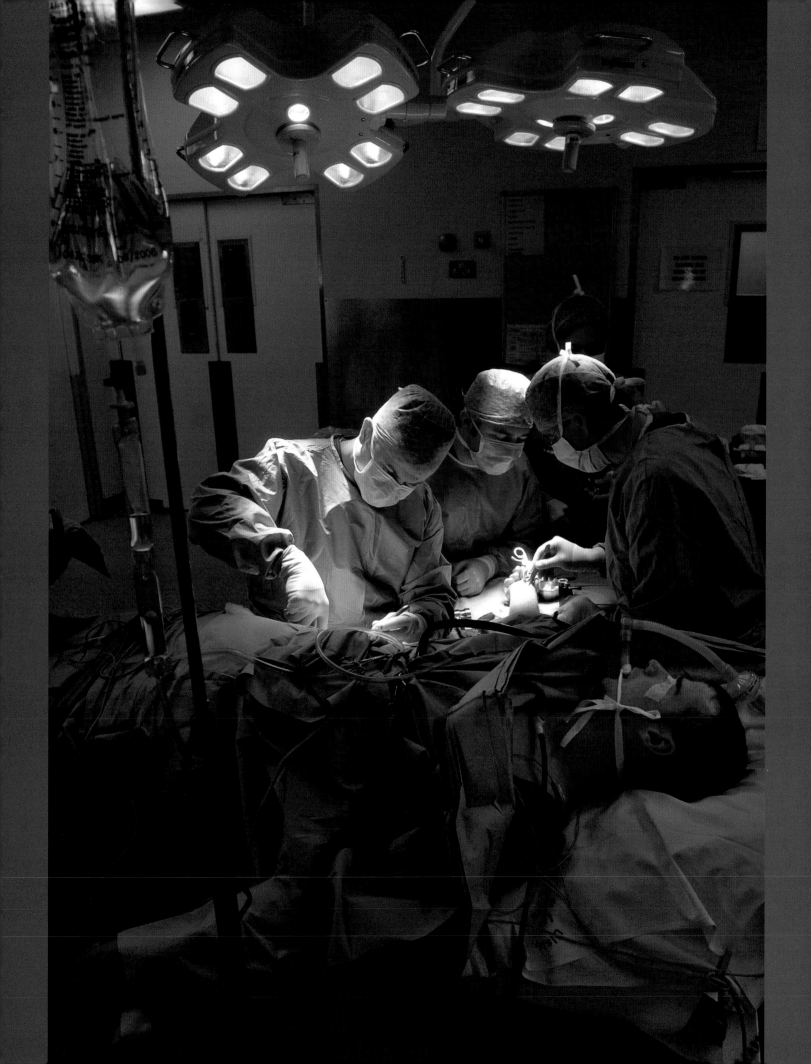

RYAN FARQUHAR, ULSTER HOSPITAL, BELFAST, 2004

Crashes and injury are occupational hazards for every competitor in any form of motorsport. In 2004 Ryan Farquhar broke his scaphoid bone in a training crash and required a bone graft from his hip to his right wrist that was carried out by surgeons in Belfast. The County Tyrone rider was back racing within a few weeks of the operation.

CAMERON DONALD, ISLE OF MAN TT, 2010

Racing six laps and over 200 miles of the TT Mountain course puts great strain on a rider's muscles and joints. Australian rider Cameron Donald damaged his shoulder in a crash at Keppel Gate during the 2009 TT and, a year on, still required treatment for the injury. On the morning of the Superbike TT he received a massage from Manx physiotherapist Isla Scott amongst his race bikes.

CONOR CUMMINS, ISLE OF MAN TT, 2012

Manxman Conor Cummins spent two years fighting his way back to fitness after sustaining terrible injuries to his back, legs and arms following a crash at the 2010 TT. After joining the Tyco Suzuki squad at the start of the 2012 season he seemed set for a promising return to racing, but his hopes were dashed when he was knocked off his bike in a crash at the North West 200 in May. He sustained two broken bones in his right hand and, rather than racing at the TT in 2012, Cummins joined the ranks of the walking wounded who hobble through the doors of the Island's hyperbaric chamber. Daily sessions in the pressurised chamber provide an increase in oxygen supply which helps to accelerate the healing of broken bones.

MICHAEL DUNLOP, ULSTER GRAND PRIX, 2012

A team of highly trained medics is on hand at every road race event to deal with rider injuries in the event of a crash. Helicopters as well as ambulances are used to transport crash victims to hospital. During the 2012 season Michael Dunlop injured his back and required painkillers before the start of each meeting to allow him to race. One of the race doctors, Dr John Hinds, administered the four injections that Dunlop received at Dundrod on the morning of the race.

MARTIN FINNEGAN, ISLE OF MAN TT, 2006
With moments to go before the start of a TT race, Martin Finnegan sits alone with his thoughts in his motorhome. The TT Mountain course offers both the greatest challenge in road racing and the most dangerous: over two hundred riders have died there in over one hundred years of competition. Finnegan lost his life in a crash at the Tandragee 100 in 2008.

GLASLOUGH, COUNTY MONAGHAN, 2004

Riders in the Junior Support class are offered encouragement as they wait at the paddock gate to be called to the grid for the start of their event at the Monaghan road races.

Race paddocks in Ireland are usually fields or yards acquired by the organising club from local farmers for the days of competition.

Road racers raise their own finance to purchase the machinery they ride, and make the bikes ready to race with the help of friends and family. Sponsorship is meagre in the sport, and only an elite few are in teams that have enough money to be able to pay riders to race. The other main types of racing income available to riders are start and prize money, but it is only those at the front of the race who benefit from this, leaving the rest of the riders to pay all of their own expenses, including the entry fees for each event.

GARY JOHNSON, ISLE OF MAN TT, 2010

Road races are held on closed public roads that include all of the paraphernalia of daily life such as bus shelters, traffic signs and garden walls. At some parts of the course, bales are put in place to offer a degree of protection to the riders in the event of a crash, but most of the hazards remain exposed.

This bus shelter on the Glencrutchery Road provides riders with a retreat from the frantic activity of the TT start line.

GLASLOUGH, COUNTY MONAGHAN, 2004

Riders stand with their machines on the grid as the
national anthem is played before the start of the
first race of the day at the Monaghan road races.

SCARBOROUGH, 2008

The pack streams through Mere Hairpin on
the opening lap of the Superbike race at the
Scarborough Gold Cup at Oliver's Mount. The
Yorkshire parkland circuit hosts the only race held
on closed public roads in Great Britain.

WILLIAM DUNLOP AND ALESSANDRO LA MACCHIA, NORTH WEST 200, 2011

The 8.9-mile North West 200 course follows a triangular network of roads that links three towns on the north coast of Northern Ireland. The long, fast straights of the open country between Coleraine and Portrush were the first places where race bikes on a circuit were recorded going at speeds of over 200 mph in the UK. From Portrush to Portstewart the road follows the coastal cliff top, passing the garden gates of the houses at Dhu Varren and the caravan parks of the holidaymakers who flock to the race in their thousands each May.

250CC RACE, MID-ANTRIM 150, 2009

The 250cc pack makes its way around the gates of St James's Church in Clough village, County Antrim, the home of the Mid-Antrim 150. The 150 refers to the distance of the original race when the event was first run in 1946. Today the races are much shorter, comprising no more than six or seven laps of the 3.6-mile circuit. There have also been several changes of circuit over the past sixty-seven years.

CORK ROAD RACES, 2013

Michael Sweeney, Michael Pearson and William Dunlop in action during the Open race at Glanmire, County Cork, in June 2013. Every road race in the world, with the exception of the Isle of Man TT, is organised and run by a small band of amateur enthusiasts. The members of the Cork Motorcycle and Vintage Club ran a series of fundraising events over two years to raise the money to bring a road race to Glanmire. Bad weather forced the cancellation of the meeting after just one race had been completed.

ULSTER GRAND PRIX, 2009

Guy Martin's Hydrex Honda is just a blur as he flashes through
Jordan's crossroads at Dundrod at over 170 mph during practice
for the 2009 Ulster Grand Prix. The venue for a round of the
Grand Prix world championship before the series moved away
from road circuits in the 1970s, the course in the hills above
Belfast is now the fastest race circuit in the world with an
average speed of over 133 mph for the 7.4 miles.

WILLIAM DUNLOP, TIMOLEAGUE, 2011

Although officials of the governing bodies of motorcycle road racing carry out
inspections and risk assessments of the roads that are to be used for racing, these
rarely, if ever, involve any testing by a rider on a bike. The Timoleague course in
West Cork was used for the first and only time in June 2011 and riders like William
Dunlop had only a few laps of practice to find the limits to which they could push
themselves and their machines at a place like O'Brien's Leap.

SHAUN ANDERSON, BUSH, 2012

The narrow country lanes of the Irish National road race courses are full of bumps and hollows that will shake everyday traffic around at normal road speeds. Once those roads are closed and the race begins, these same features – at places like the Spade Mill on the Bush circuit – become huge jumps for riders like Shaun Anderson on his 600cc Suzuki.

Anderson crashed later in the race, breaking his leg.

KEITH AMOR, KELLS, 2009

Spectators watch Keith Amor jump Hanlon's Leap on his Craig Honda at Kells road races in County Meath. The event was one of the most popular in the Irish calendar, attracting some of the biggest names in the sport, but the economic difficulties facing the Republic of Ireland meant that the 2011 race was the last to be run. In both 2009 and 2010 riders were killed in crashes at Kells.

'If you let the slightest bit
of doubt creep into your
mind then you'll be dead.
I like stuff like that.'

DUNMANWAY, COUNTY CORK, 2010

After a gap of eighteen years, the Munster 100 road races were revived on the streets of Dunmanway in August 2010. The organisers of the event promoted the new race by referencing its historic past, in particular Joey Dunlop's and Philip McCallen's previous involvement. Unique in that it ran through the streets of the town as well as on the roads in the countryside, the organisers placed over nine hundred safety bales along the route. At one stage the possibility of deploying an inflated bouncy castle in a river beside the track in case of an accident was also considered.

The race was shifted to another circuit in nearby Timoleague the following year.

DUNMANWAY SPRINT, COUNTY CORK, 2012

A race fan checks the entry list in the programme for the Dunmanway Sprint.

JOHN BURROWS, TANDRAGEE 100, 2011

The Tandragee 100 has been run on the same course since its inception in 1958. At 5.3 miles, the County Armagh circuit is the longest of the Irish national road races. Newer courses tend to be about only half the length – the shorter circuits are easier to manage as there are usually fewer residents along the route, and they require fewer marshals and medics.

Flag marshals, who wear white coats and are always placed within sight of a colleague behind and in front, use different coloured flags to warn riders of any hazards or crashes that may be on the road ahead.

WILLIAM DUNLOP, ATHEA, 2011

The road is so narrow at this point on the 3.3-mile Athea circuit in County Limerick that the lines are painted along the edges of the tarmac instead of down the middle of the road so that drivers know where the grass verge begins.

PAUL MAGUIRE, ATHEA, 2008

When a road is chosen as part of the route of a road race, the club and the inspection team from the governing body – who will provide the permit for competition – have to work with what they find there, whether it be houses and telegraph poles or holy wells and shrines, such as here at Athea in County Limerick.

Paul Maguire was badly injured in a crash at Athea in 2006 but recovered and returned to racing.

The Athea road race has not run since 2011.

WAYNE KENNEDY, DUNMANWAY, COUNTY CORK, 2010

Almost all of the motorcycles currently competing in road racing are based on street bikes. Specially manufactured racing machines such as the 250cc Honda that Wayne Kennedy was racing at Dunmanway in 2010 have been phased out of world championship racing and their numbers continue to diminish in road racing.

BLAIR DEGERHOLM, ULSTER GRAND PRIX, 2000

Attempts have been made to reduce speeds on sections of some Irish courses by implementing artificial chicanes. Although these chicanes have the effect of slowing the riders down, they have also been the scene of crashes, including some that have been fatal.

Road racers say the challenge is in dealing with the course as they find it, complete with all of the obstacles that present dangers.

Blair Degerholm's racing career ended after he was injured in a racing crash at Donington Park.

SEAMUS ELLIOTT AND JAMIE HAMILTON, MID-ANTRIM 150, 2013

Most road races in Ireland are run around small villages
or towns like Clough in County Antrim, home of the
Mid-Antrim 150. Traditionally the finance to run these
events has come from local private businesses such
as car dealers, builders' merchants, shops and pubs. As
costs have risen, clubs have been forced to look for
new sources of revenue and some have begun to market
their spectacular events as tourist attractions, receiving
support from tourism bodies and local councils. With
this public funding has come more intense scrutiny of
the way these races are run and pressure is growing on
amateur race officials to comply with ever more stringent
health and safety procedures.

DEAN HARRISON, ARMOY, 2010

Although road racing in Ireland – particularly in the Republic – has been badly affected by the economic recession of recent years, the passion and enthusiasm for the sport remain as strong as ever, as events like Armoy road races highlight. Events at Athea, Bush and Kells have now disappeared from the calendar but the Armoy races have gone from strength to strength since their inception in 2009.

The small County Antrim village was the home of the legendary 'Armoy Armada', four local riders who had a huge following in the 1970s. The modern races have drawn on this connection with Joey and Jim Dunlop, Frank Kennedy and Mervyn Robinson to link the past with the present and to tap into a romantic legacy of the sport that has captured the imagination of race fans. The current Clerk of the Course is Frank Kennedy's brother Bill, and the feature race of the day is called 'The Race of Legends', but the nostalgic link has been most strongly represented by the inclusion in the starting line-up at Armoy of William, Michael and Sam Dunlop and their cousin Paul Robinson. Paul is the son of Armada member Mervyn Robinson and all four riders are the nephews of the most famous Armada racer, Joey Dunlop.

Jim Dunlop was awarded a lifetime honorary membership of the Armoy club in 2013 but sadly Frank Kennedy, Mervyn Robinson and Joey Dunlop have all lost their lives in racing crashes.

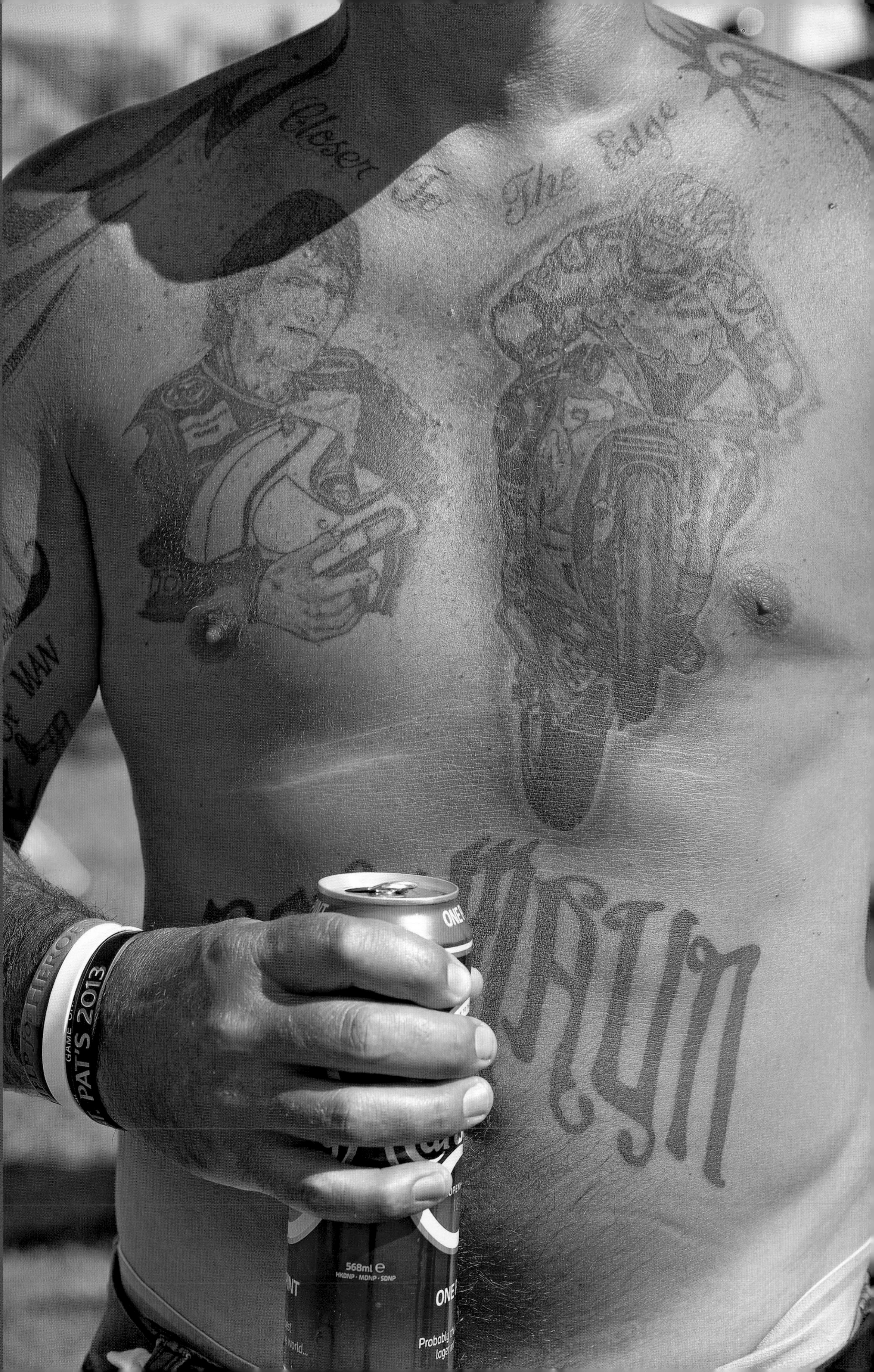
Closer To The Edge
PAT'S 2013
568ml

RACE FAN, SOUTHERN 100, 2013

RACE FAN, NORTH WEST 200, 2013

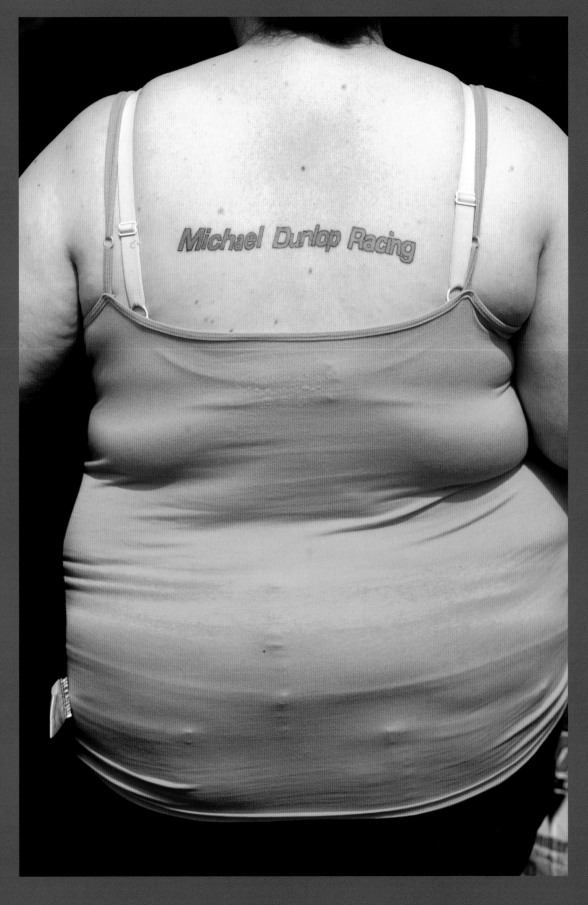

'There's just me, the stopwatch and the track. There is no room for excuses.'

JOHN McGUINNESS
NORTH WEST 200, 2012

SCARBOROUGH, 2009

As the only road race in England, the Oliver's Mount parkland circuit attracts large crowds every year. The Gold Cup event, held each September, is the main race of the season at the Yorkshire track.

Where road racers choose to compete is largely a matter of personal preference. Apart from the North West 200, the Isle of Man TT and the Ulster Grand Prix, which are the main International road races, there are very few other events that are attended by all of the British and Irish riders who race on the roads. Many Irish riders, for instance, do not race at Scarborough, and racers like John McGuinness or Ian Hutchinson, who regularly compete at Oliver's Mount, rarely race on the Irish National circuits.

The majority of motorcycle racers who confine their racing to the purpose-built short circuit tracks never compete in road races although there are exceptions, as well as contradictions. Barry Sheene, Britain's last 500cc world champion, was a vociferous opponent of pure road racing because of the dangers associated with it, but he was a regular competitor at Oliver's Mount throughout the 1970s and '80s.

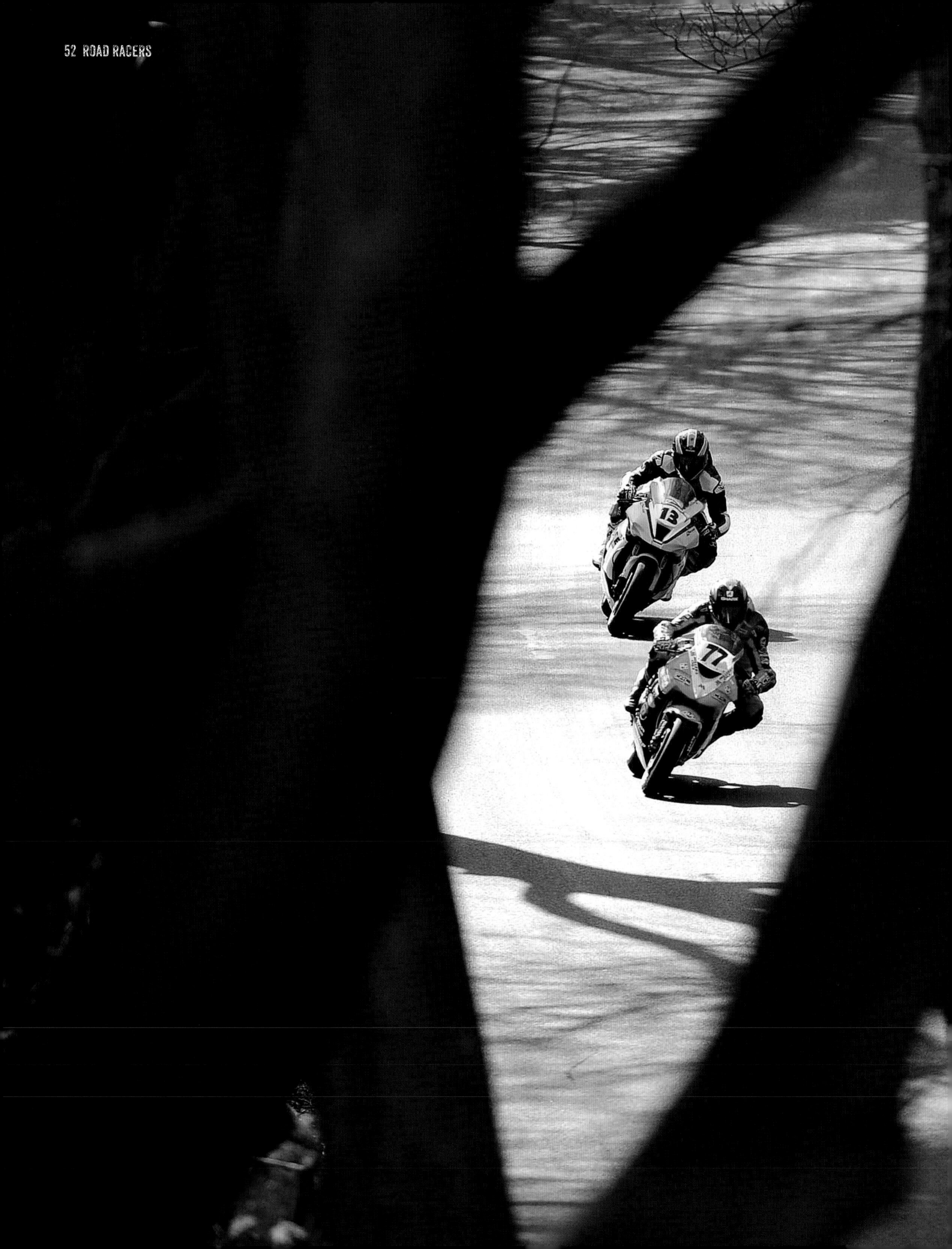

RYAN FARQUHAR AND ADRIAN ARCHIBALD, SCARBOROUGH, 2012

Riders from every part of the world compete in races like the Isle of Man TT and the Macau Grand Prix in China but the vast majority of those who compete in road races on a regular basis come from Ireland and the UK.

Ryan Farquhar and Adrian Archibald, both from Northern Ireland, retired in 2012 after long and successful careers that saw them win TTs as well as races at Scarborough and on most courses in Ireland.

CHRIS PALMER, SCARBOROUGH, 2012

A two-stroke specialist who won a total of ninety-seven races at
Scarborough during his career, Chris Palmer retired from racing at the
Gold Cup meeting at Oliver's Mount in 2013. Many of Palmer's race
battles were fought out against his contemporary, Ian Lougher, who
retired from the sport on the same day.

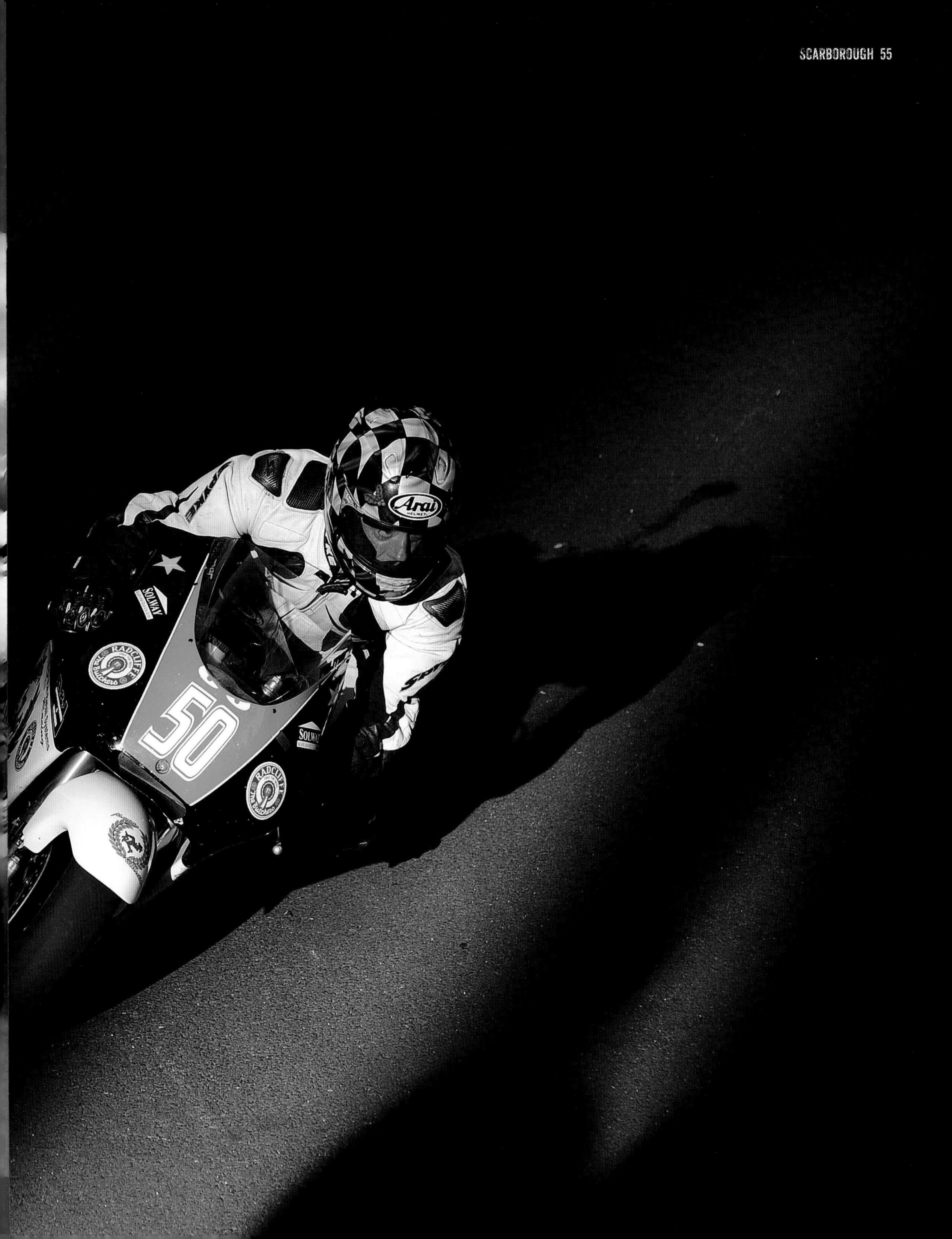

CLASSIC RACE, HORICE, CZECH REPUBLIC, 2011

After passing through the town of Horice, the 300 Zatacek Gustav Havel course climbs uphill to this pine forest section. Havel was a leading Czech racer of the '50s and '60s who won at the first race meeting run on the 3.2-mile Horice course in 1962. Another Czech road race, held at Terlicko, forms a round of the International Road Racing Championship, which also includes races on road circuits in Belgium and Germany.

MICHAEL PEARSON, HORICE, CZECH REPUBLIC, 2011

In 2011 two local racers were killed at Horice when they collided on the approach to the forest at the top of the circuit. The inclusion of this tree-lined area as part of the Horice track means it is impossible for the organisers to offer much protection, beyond the occasional straw bale tied to a tree, to the riders in the event of a crash. It was on a section of track almost identical to this that Joey Dunlop lost his life in Estonia in 2000 when he slid off his 125cc Honda in the wet.

HORICE 65

MICHAEL PEARSON, DEAN HARRISON AND IVAN LINTIN, SOUTHERN 100, 2012
Whether it is run through the forests of Horice or between the walls
at Billown, there is very little margin for error in any road race.

GUY MARTIN, PRE-TT CLASSIC, BILLOWN, ISLE OF MAN, 2008

The Pre-TT Classic and post-TT meetings, which bookend the Isle of Man TT races, are both run on the 4.25-mile Billown circuit near Castletown. Billown also plays host to the Southern 100 event each July.

Unlike modern MotoGP or World Superbike riders, who only ride in one class and on one bike, many road racers compete on a wide variety of machinery across various classes. Some even race on Classic bikes, such as the '70s era Suzuki that Guy Martin is racing here.

MICHAEL DUNLOP, SOUTHERN 100, 2013

Michael Dunlop shaves the wall as he wheelies past Joey's Gate during the opening practice session for the Southern 100.

The gate at Ballanorris bend is named after Michael's uncle, Joey Dunlop, who ran wide on the exit of the corner during a race in 1979 and could only avoid a crash by steering through the gate into the adjoining field.

MICHAEL DUNLOP, SOUTHERN 100, 2011

Dunlop exits the same corner in the 600cc race at the Southern 100 two years earlier. He has dominated the meeting in recent years, winning three races in 2011, five in 2012 and two in 2013.

RUSS MOUNTFORD, SOUTHERN 100, 2012

Riders try to play down the dangers
presented by the stone walls of the
Billown course with characteristic
black humour.

'It's not so bad because there are
only two walls,' they say, 'one on
the left and one on the right, all
the way round.'

The safety bales that line the
outside of corners like Church Bend
offer the racers some protection,
but riders often touch their
shoulders against the wall on the
inside of the bend.

Fascinated by the gladiatorial
spectacle, racegoers occupy a safe
vantage point in the graveyard
beside the road, separated from the
unfathomable dangers by two feet
of solid rock.

LA BAÑEZA, SPAIN, 2012

Every August since 1954, during the festival of the
Annunciation of the Virgin Mary, the small Castilian
town of La Bañeza has been the venue for the Gran
Premio de La Bañeza, Spain's only road race.

Four races – for two- and four-stroke Classic bikes
and for production and Grand Prix 125cc machines
– are run around the town's narrow streets where
over twenty thousand people line the pavements
to watch the action.

CLASSIC RACE, LA BAÑEZA, SPAIN, 2012

Safety measures are at a minimum and spectators are permitted to stand almost anywhere as the four-stroke Classic machines race through the streets.

Spanish riders like Dani Pedrosa, Jorge Lorenzo and Marc Márquez, who now dominate MotoGP racing, will not be found competing at La Bañeza – they stick to the purpose-built racetracks at Jerez, Barcelona and Catalunya. But in the past, Spanish world champions like Ángel Nieto and Jorge Martínez did race on the 1.75-mile street circuit.

125CC RACE, LA BAÑEZA, SPAIN, 2012

Practice takes place on Saturday evening as revellers arrive to take part in the festival. By Sunday, with over twenty thousand people lining the course, the races are run through a human tunnel.

AITOR CREMADES FLORES, LA BAÑEZA, SPAIN, 2012

The Spanish fans catch the last of the day's sunshine as they get a close-up view of Aitor Cremades Flores during the GP125 practice on Saturday evening.

125CC PRACTICE, LA BAÑEZA, SPAIN, 2012
Although race organisers have tried
to minimise the likelihood of serious
accidents by limiting the size of the
machines taking part in the races and
by introducing some safety measures,
La Bañeza still feels like a remnant
of the old days. Invented before the
term 'health and safety' ever entered
sporting parlance, the race continues as
if such strictures still do not exist.

ALEXANDRO MARTÍNEZ MAS, LA BAÑEZA, SPAIN, 2012
Spanish racer, Alexandro Martínez Mas, was the runaway
winner of the feature race at La Bañeza in 2012.

LA BAÑEZA, SPAIN, 2012

The Spanish post-race celebrations involve an invasion of fans onto the racetrack during the slowing-down lap. Exuberant spectators throw their hats on the road for the riders to run over.

RACE FAN, KILLALANE ROAD RACES, 2010

In Ireland, unlike the Isle of Man or Scarborough, spectators are allowed to move around the track between races to find new vantage points. With his rucksack hanging in the hedge, a race fan at Killalane has declined the opportunity and opted to take a nap instead.

Both Killalane and Skerries are run by the same organising club, and the County Dublin courses share a short section of road. Run at the beginning of September, Killalane is the final race in the Irish road racing calendar.

DAN STEWART, ISLE OF MAN TT, 2010

As bikes have become faster and more evenly matched, TT races are now being won by a few seconds or even fractions of a second, rather than in minutes, which was much more the norm twenty and more years ago. As every rider pushes for that extra tenth of a second, the riding has become more extreme, especially at places like Ballaugh Bridge.

YOSHINARI MATSUSHITA , ISLE OF MAN TT, 2011

The Japanese racer and journalist got his big
break in racing in 2013 when he agreed terms
with the successful Tyco Suzuki team to race
a GSXR600 at the TT.

I photographed Matsushita in the Tyco garage
just as the race bike he would ride was
unveiled at 3 p.m. on the day that practice
began. He was delighted and very excited to
be getting the chance to race the factory-
prepared machine.

On the second lap of practice, at 7.45 p.m. that
evening, Matsushita crashed at Ballacrye at
over 150 mph. He was killed instantly.

CONOR CUMMINS, ISLE OF MAN TT, 2010

It is a measure of the mental strength of a road racer, especially those who compete at the very highest level, to be able to push aside the constant threat of injury and totally commit to every corner. It is an even greater challenge for the rider to make that commitment if he has suffered a serious injury following a crash.

In 2010, Manxman Conor Cummins' McAdoo Kawasaki ZX10 slid off the road at The Verandah on the Mountain section of the TT course and fired him down the side of Snaefell. His body was shattered in the crash, and he required years of surgery and physiotherapy to recover. Only Cummins knows exactly how deep the mental scars of the trauma have cut, but he has now returned to racing.

In 2012 and 2013 he regularly scored podium finishes at the big international road races, including the TT.

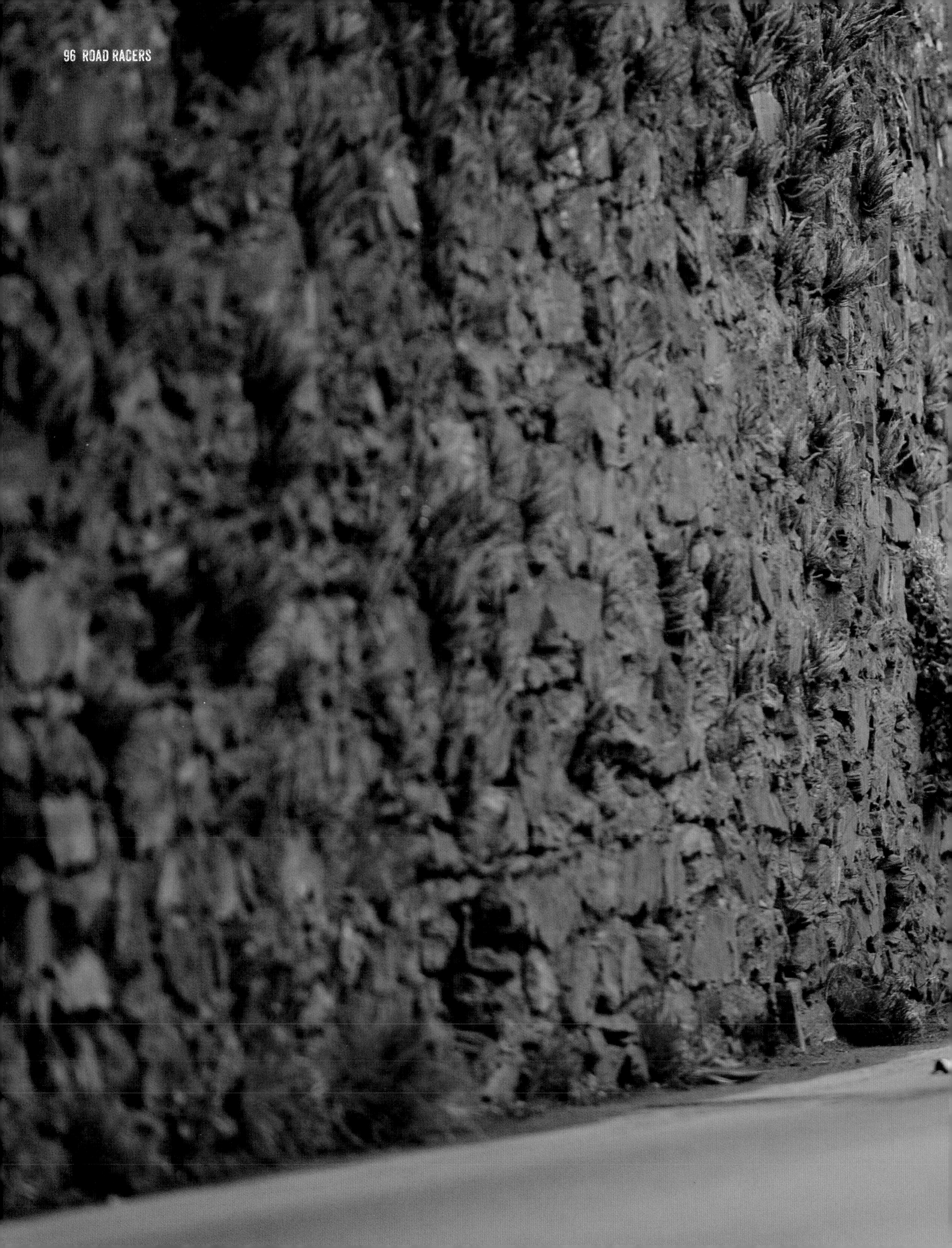

GUY MARTIN, ISLE OF MAN TT, 2012

The combination of extreme length and high-speed corners makes the Isle of Man TT course a daunting prospect for every road racer. At places like Handley's Bend, the looming stone walls provide an unforgiving reminder of the dangers, though riders will often say that they are oblivious to their surroundings as they concentrate on the patch of tarmac just ahead of their front wheel. This intense concentration has a mesmeric effect on a rider, allowing him to shut out the obvious perils as he attempts to pull every corner into a seamless smooth thread.

JOHN McGUINNESS, ISLE OF MAN TT, 2013

St Ninian's crossroads is less than half a mile from the TT start line. Ordinarily, during the fifty weeks of the year when the TT races are not in progress, it is a busy junction controlled by traffic lights. Nine times out of ten you would probably have to stop and wait for the green light to appear before you could pass through.

But for two weeks in June, when the roads are closed, John McGuinness and the rest of the frontrunners in the Superbike and Senior TTs pass through St Ninian's at over 170 mph.

KEITH AMOR, ISLE OF MAN TT, 2010

During early morning practice for the 1927 TT, Archie Birkin met a fish van travelling towards Peel, close to this spot outside Kirkmichael village. Birkin swerved to avoid the van but lost control of his machine and suffered a fatal crash.

Incredible as it may seem, in those far-off days, practice for the TT was carried out on the open highway but from 1928, following Birkin's death, the roads were closed for practice as well as racing. Then and now, the implementation of safety features in road racing has been a largely reactive process.

JOHN McGUINNESS, ISLE OF MAN TT, 2013

Since racing began on the Mountain course in 1911, four years after the advent of TT racing itself, lap speeds have risen relentlessly. Machine and course improvements and the appearance of especially gifted riders have provided the momentum for the continuous improvement.

Between 1924 and 1932, Jimmy Simpson was the first man to break the 60, 70 and 80 mph barriers. Harold Daniell, a man whose eyesight was so poor that he was rejected for military service during the Second World War, set the first sub-25-minute lap at over 91 mph in 1938.

Not until 1957 was the landmark 100 mph limit exceeded by Bob McIntyre, and it was another five years before Gary Hocking hit a 105 mph average.

In 1976 John Williams was the first to raise the bar over 110 mph and Joey Dunlop was the first to better 115 mph in 1980.

By the end of the decade, in 1989, Steve Hislop had established the first 120 mph lap and the new millennium saw David Jefferies break the 125 mph limit in 2000.

John McGuinness became the outright lap record holder for the Mountain course in 2004 and the Morecambe rider has maintained his position as the fastest man on the Mountain since. In 2007, the centenary of TT racing, he set the first 130 mph lap and in 2013 he established a new benchmark of 131.671 mph.

'I was brought up with
racing: I've been in the
paddock since I was born.
I don't know anything else.'

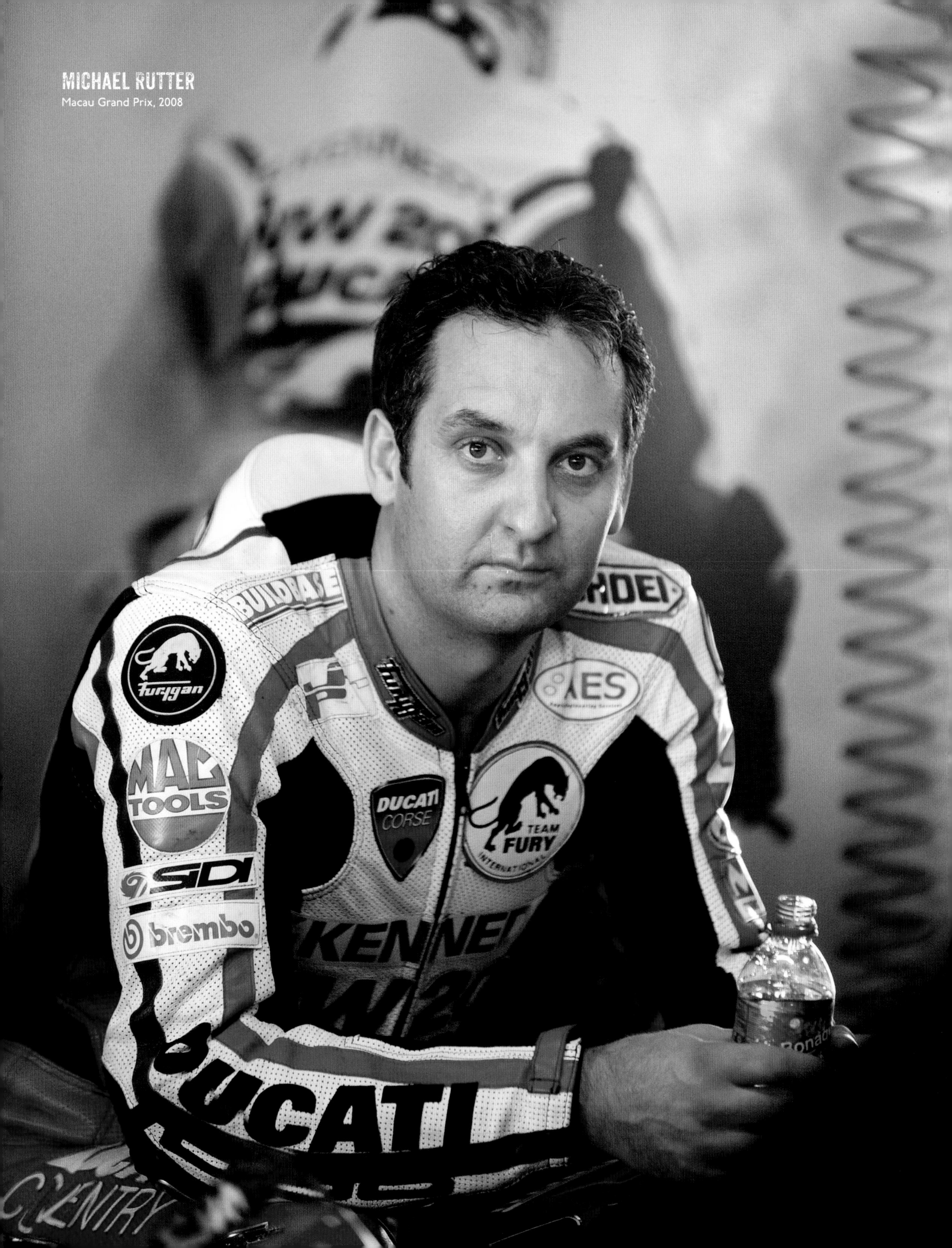

MICHAEL RUTTER
Macau Grand Prix, 2008

CONOR CUMMINS, MACAU GRAND PRIX, 2012

The Chinese city of Macau is the only city in the world that plays host to motorcycle racing on its streets and the dangers that this setting presents are stark. The 3.8-mile Guia circuit in the former Portuguese colony is lined with Armco barriers and concrete walls.

MICHAEL RUTTER, MACAU GRAND PRIX, 2008

A sideshow to the Formula 3 car event that dominates proceedings at Macau, the bike race was traditionally regarded as an end-of-season holiday wind-down for the two-wheeled fraternity.

Over the last decade the event has become intensely competitive with all of the world's top road racers travelling to China seeking a Macau win. The race is now regarded as a top International event alongside the North West 200, Isle of Man TT and Ulster Grand Prix.

CAMERON DONALD, MACAU GRAND PRIX, 2008
Australian double TT winner Cameron Donald describes
riding this part of the Macau course, the twisty hill top
section, as like 'threading the needle'.

KEITH AMOR, MACAU GRAND PRIX, 2008

'There is absolutely no rest at all in Macau – you are always preparing yourself for the next corner. This is a scary place and if you turn in too early you are in real danger of becoming the ball in a mad pinball game as you bounce off the barriers and walls.'

Keith Amor on racing at Macau.

IAN HUTCHINSON, MACAU GRAND PRIX, 2011

Some Macau riders say that they prefer to race closer to the smooth concrete walls rather than to the Armco barriers, which have protruding bolt heads that can rip their leathers if they catch on them.

STEFANO BONNETTI, MACAU GRAND PRIX, 2012

The price paid for any error at Macau can be extremely high. Italian rider Stefano Bonnetti's right front brake calliper appeared to come off his Suzuki as he braked at the bottom of Moorish Hill during the opening practice session in 2012. One of the retaining bolts can be seen in the air above his left knee.

Bonnetti suffered extensive injuries after crashing into the barrier, including fractures to his lower back, ribs and right foot, and a broken left thigh bone.

Later the same day Portuguese rider Luis Carreira lost his life in a crash at Fisherman's Bend.

MARSHAL, MACAU GRAND PRIX, 2005
A marshal takes a nap during race day.

SIMON ANDREWS, MACAU GRAND PRIX, 2012

In June 2012 Simon Andrews was badly injured in a high-speed crash at the Isle of Man TT.

'I had to learn to walk again and repair nerve damage, a badly broken wrist, shoulder, scapular, ribs, ankle, dislocated shoulder, fingers, thumb and ruptured eyes,' he recalls.

With his injuries not fully healed, Andrews made his road racing comeback at Macau in November and finished on the podium.

MICHAEL RUTTER, MACAU GRAND PRIX, 2012

Street lamps cast an orange glow on
the road as Michael Rutter climbs San
Francisco Hill in the dim light of early
morning practice. Rutter is the most
successful rider of all time at Macau – he
took his eighth win in 2012.

BRIAN McCORMACK, DUNMANWAY SPRINT, 2012

Road racing remains a sport where on-track rivalries are set aside and competitors socialise together after the chequered flag drops. The paddock community is often described as a family; one that enjoys the camaraderie of a travelling band but closes ranks to offer support to those who suffer difficult times.

It is also a place that is full of fun, shared amongst people who spend a large part of their lives on the road together in pursuit of an aspiration that few people outside the sport can fathom.

MICHAEL DUNLOP, ISLE OF MAN TT, 2012

It is probable that Stanley Woods is the youngest ever
TT winner but, as the birth certificate of the legendary
Dublin rider cannot be traced, it is impossible to be
certain. Mike Hailwood also laid claim to the accolade
when he won his first TT at twenty-one in 1961.

When Michael Dunlop won his first TT race in 2009 it
was thought that he was also twenty-one and slightly
older than Hailwood had been. But the Ballymoney rider
was actually only twenty years old. The confusion had
been caused by the fact that his father had added a year
to his son's age on the application for his race licence so
that Michael could begin his racing career a year earlier
than was legally allowed.

Regardless of the specifics of his date of birth, it is clear
that Michael Dunlop is a prodigious talent. A winner at
all three of the major International road races, the Irish
rider took his total tally of Island wins to seven in 2013,
winning four TT races in one week to establish himself
as the foremost rider of his generation.

GARY JOHNSON, ISLE OF MAN TT, 2011

Gary Johnson uses the winner's cap to wipe sweat
from his brow after winning the Supersport TT in 2011.

WILLIAM DUNLOP, ISLE OF MAN TT, 2012

William Dunlop cannot hide his disappointment after
finishing third in the Supersport race at the 2012 TT.

WILLIAM DAVISON, BELLAGHY, 2013

William Davison broke his neck in a crash at Tournagrough during practice for the Ulster Grand Prix in 2013. The halo brace, which is attached by four bolts that are screwed directly into his skull, keeps his head straight. He has to wear it for three months before doctors can decide whether or not surgery is required to mend the broken vertebrae.

No matter what the outcome, Davison has decided never to race again for fear that another crash would damage his weakened neck and leave him with the paralysis he was lucky to escape in this crash.

RYAN FARQUHAR, COUNTY TYRONE, 2012

Wearing his racing leathers, Ryan Farquhar helps carry the coffin of his uncle, Trevor Ferguson, as his body is returned from the Isle of Man to his home in County Tyrone.

Ferguson died after crashing during a race at the Manx Grand Prix in August 2012.

The pair had shared a close bond throughout their racing careers. Trevor had taken Farquhar to races as a child and provided the bike that he rode in his first road race.

On the day of his death Ferguson had been riding one of Farquhar's bikes and Farquhar had been waiting to help refuel it during the pitstop at the end of the second lap.

Ryan Farquhar announced his retirement from the sport after Trevor's death and has not competed since.

PAUL ROBINSON, NORTH WEST 200, 2010

Mervyn Robinson was one of the legendary quartet of 1970s riders known as the Armoy Armada. He lost his life in a crash at the North West 200 in 1980.

Thirty years after his father's death, Paul Robinson won the 125cc race at the 2010 event. It was his first win on the circuit and the last ever 125cc race to be held there.

The following day Paul laid his winner's laurels on his father's grave.

WILLIAM AND MICHAEL DUNLOP AND BARRY DAVIDSON, MID-ANTRIM 150, 2009

When Michael Dunlop won four races at the TT in 2013 his total
winnings in prize money were over £60,000. The entire prize fund
for the eight races run at the 2009 Mid-Antrim 150 was £9,000 and
Michael's brother William would have received several hundred
pounds as the winner of the 250cc race.

IAN HUTCHINSON, SCARBOROUGH, 2010

In 2010 Ian Hutchinson enjoyed a season of unparalleled success.
A winner at the North West 200 and the Ulster Grand Prix, it was his
clean sweep of all five of the main TT races on the Isle of Man that
provided the glittering highlight of the Yorkshire man's *annus mirabilis*.

By winning his local road race at Scarborough in September's Gold
Cup meeting Hutchinson put the seal on the finest pure road racing
season in history. But just one week later he crashed in the rain during
a British championship race at a short-circuit meeting at Silverstone.
Hutchinson was run over as he lay on the track, suffering a compound
fracture to his left leg that was so serious that doctors initially
considered amputation.

After more than twenty operations and three years of treatment and
physiotherapy, Hutchinson intends to return to racing.

'That is what I do and that is what I want to do again,' he said.

'I just want to win, nothing else matters.'

MICHAEL DUNLOP
ISLE OF MAN TT, 2013

To the victor the spoils. Bedecked with the winner's laurels, Michael Dunlop walks away with the champagne and the famous Winged Mercury trophy having just won the 2013 Superbike TT.

PHIL ARCHER, ATHEA, 2004

'The best part of a road race is getting
into the van to go home.' JOEY DUNLOP

First published in 2013 by Blackstaff Press, 4D Weavers Court, Linfield Road, Belfast BT12 5GH, Northern Ireland

Reprinted 2014

Text © Stephen Davison, 2013

Photographs © Stephen Davison/Pacemaker Press International, 2013

All rights reserved

Stephen Davison has asserted his right under the Copyright, Designs and Patents Act 1988 to be identified as the author of this work.

Designed by seagulls.net

Printed by Rotolito Lombardo

A CIP catalogue record for this book is available from the British Library

ISBN 978-085640-914-1

www.blackstaffpress.com

www.pacemakerpressintl.com